THE BI

MW01268580

A Comprehensive Outline for Study of the Entire
Sacred Volume

By

Rev. G. Campbell Morgan D. D.

Fleming H. Revell Company
1922

CROSSREACH PUBLICATIONS

Hope. Inspiration. Trust.

CONTENTS

GENERAL INTRODUCTION

THESE LESSONS ARE suggestive merely. The arrangement is intended to give a course whereby the student shall gain a comprehensive knowledge of the Bible as a whole. In the study and teaching much will be required which is not supplied in this pamphlet. That may be obtained in general literature bearing on the subjects. Thirty-nine lessons are arranged for each year so as to leave three months for vacation periods, and Sundays on which the Festivals of the Church will be the subject of teaching, Christmas, Easter, and others.

In all teaching a matter of fundamental importance is that we should know the material with which we have to deal, both as to the subject to be considered, and the stage reached in the mental development of those to be taught.

In the period of youth, from fifteen or sixteen years and upward, all the faculties-the intellectual, the emotional, and the volitional-are tending toward consistency and balanced activity. The working of the will is now seeking for reasons for its choices; and yielding to the inspirations of emotion. This is the time when no side of the complex nature must be neglected, as everything is rapidly tending toward a consistent and poised attitude of life, which may be wholly good or wholly bad.

The hour has now come in which students are ready to receive the whole Bible. This, however, should be done with a distinct understanding in the mind of the teacher, that the central and final value of the Bible is Christ Himself. I am more and more convinced in my study and teaching of the Word of God, that whereas it is not ours to choose, and say that certain portions of the Bible are on a higher level of inspiration than others, it is ours to distinguish the difference between shadow and substance; between the finger-posts that direct men toward the city of God, and the city of God itself; between the divers portions and divers places of the Old, and the unified and final speech of the New. We have to introduce our students to the whole Library, and to the central Person, showing the relation between the two.

In the teaching of the Bible at this period it is necessary that we recognize two main qualities, those namely of the history it chronicles, and of the teaching it records.

In dealing with Old Testament history our work is to show that the first meaning and value of Biblical history is that it is a revelation of the activity of God. Its progress is the program of God. Its persons are the instruments of God. Its events constitute the mosaic of God.

In considering the teaching, in every case this must have its historic setting. By observing this principle it will be possible to show the development in revelation, which is so marked a feature of the Divine Library. I hold it to be of supreme importance therefore, that in our arrangement, some portion of the literature dealing exclusively with the Person of Christ and His mission, should be studied in each year.

This method of the study of the Bible is only possible at the stage when all the elemental faculties of the mind are coming into full play. Its value is that through it we come to the discovery of the grace and government of God as ultimately revealed through Christ, this being the true principle upon which these elemental faculties are rendered consistent and balanced.

G. Campbell Morgan.

FIRST YEAR

THE PENTATEUCH
THE LAWS OF ISRAEL
THE GOSPEL ACCORDING TO MARK

INTRODUCTORY NOTE

IN THE STUDY of the books of the Pentateuch we are conscious of the element of continuity in the story which they have to tell. In sequence, the history of man is traced in his relation to God, in its earliest stages; and as a whole, it reveals most clearly the need for redemption. The period is divided by outstanding personalities; Adam, Abraham, Moses.

After the redemption of the Hebrew people from Egyptian slavery, they were Divinely organized as a nation under the government of God. This organization was twofold, consisting of a great system of worship, and of a code of Laws. The laws of Israel were all religious, and the morality insisted upon was spiritual. The constitution of the nation was distinctly a Theocracy. All the laws for the government of its life were those of its King, Jehovah. In dealing with these laws we discover a development, the whole of which it is necessary to recognize, before proceeding to particular consideration of the different parts. In the study of the Pentateuch we see that its central value is the account it gives of the creation of a nation in human history, for the fulfillment of the Divine purpose of redemption. In our study of the laws of Israel we see how these laws relate religion to life by providing a way of worship and a code of ethics; but they leave the people with a consciousness of sin, and confidence in God.

Our studies are completed by passing over the intervening centuries, to the Gospel of Jesus Christ, the Son of God; and in teaching, our business is to observe how the need revealed in the Old Testament has been met in Christ.

A. THE PENTATEUCH

LESSON 1. Adam to Abraham. Beginnings. Genesis 1-4

LESSON 2. Adam to Abraham. Race Developments. Genesis 5-6:9

LESSON 3. Abraham to Moses. The elect Man. Genesis 11:10-20

LESSON 4. Abraham to Moses. The elect Seed. Genesis 21-36

LESSON 5. Abraham to Moses. The elect Son. Genesis 37-45

LESSON 6. Abraham to Moses. The elect People. Genesis 46-51

LESSON 7. Moses. The Exodus. Exodus 2-15:21

C. THE GOSPEL ACCORDING TO MARK

G. CAMPBELL MORGAN

G. CAMPBELL MORGAN

G. CAMPBELL MORGAN

LESSON 35. Service. Commission of Twelve and Service. 6:7-8:30

LESSON 36. Sacrifice. Anticipated. 8:31-10

LESSON 37. Sacrifice. Approached. 11-14:11

LESSON 38. Sacrifice. Accomplished. 14:12-15

LESSON 39. Sacrifice. Announced. 16

SECOND YEAR

THE DIRECT THEOCRACY AND ONE KINGDOM

THE BOOKS OF WISDOM AND WORSHIP

THE GOSPEL ACCORDING TO MATTHEW

INTRODUCTORY NOTE

THE PERIOD OF History to be surveyed in this year's course of lessons is that between the death of Moses and the death of Solomon. The history follows immediately upon that of the Pentateuch, tracing the story of Israel from the end of the wilderness wanderings to the dark hour preceding the disruption of the kingdom. The need is revealed for true governmental authority.

The didactic study consists of a general survey of the Wisdom and Worship books of the Old Testament. These lessons form a condensation and adaptation of the outlines in the Analyzed Bible.

The study is completed by passing over the intervening centuries to the goal; the Son of David, the Son of Abraham; listening to the voice of the One to Whom all authority is given in heaven and on earth. Again the

G. CAMPBELL MORGAN

lessons are a condensation of the outlines in the Analyzed Bible, and messages of the Books of the Bible.

A. THE DIRECT THEOCRACY AND ONE KINGDOM

LESSON 1. Under Joshua. Appointment, Invasion and Conquest. Joshua 1-12

LESSON 2. Under Joshua. Partition and Farewell. Joshua 13-14

LESSON 3. Under the Judges. Elements of Disruption and Process of Disintegration. Judges 1-8:32

LESSON 4. Under the Judges. Process of Disintegration and Parenthesis of Illustration. Judges 8:33-21

LESSON 5. Under the Judges. The Divine Arrest. 1 Samuel 1-7

LESSON 6. The One Kingdom. Saul. 1 Samuel 8-15

LESSON 7. The One Kingdom. The Divine Reign. Saul and David. 1 Samuel 16-20

LESSON 8. The One Kingdom. Saul and David. 1 Samuel 21-31

LESSON 9. The One Kingdom. David. Coming into the Kingdom. 2 Samuel 1-9

LESSON 10. The One Kingdom. David. Failure and Adversity. 2 Samuel 10-20

LESSON 11. The One Kingdom. David. Parenthesis of Illustration. 2 Samuel 21-24

LESSON 12. The One Kingdom. Solomon. 1 Kings 1-11

B. THE BOOKS OF WISDOM AND WORSHIP

LESSON 13. Job. Prologue. Controversy between Heaven and Hell. Controversy between Job and Friends. Their Coming. Job 1-3

LESSON 14. Job. Controversy between Job and Friends. First Cycle. Job 4-14

LESSON 15. Job. Controversy between Job and Friends. Second Cycle. Job 15-21

LESSON 16. Job. Controversy between Job and Friends. Third Cycle. Job 22-31

LESSON 17. Job. The Last Voice. Controversy between Jehovah and Job. Epilogue. Job 32-42

LESSON 18. Psalms. The Book of Worship. Introductory. Psalms.

LESSON 19. Psalms. Book I. Psalms 1-41

LESSON 20. Psalms. Book II. Psalms 42-82

LESSON 21. Psalms. Book III. Psalms 83-89

LESSON 22. Psalms. Book IV. Psalms 90-106

LESSON 23. Psalms. Book V. Psalms 107-150

C. THE GOSPEL ACCORDING TO MATTHEW

THIRD YEAR

HISTORIC AND PROPHETIC STUDIES
THE GOSPEL ACCORDING TO LUKE

INTRODUCTORY NOTE

THE HISTORY FOR this year is that of the break-up of the Hebrew monarchy, from the death of Solomon to the establishment of the remnant under Nehemiah. It was the period of degenerate kingship, and consequent deterioration of the nation and the national witness.

Here the order of the prophets arose, as the direct representatives of the kingship of Jehovah, and consequently as interpreters of His Kingdom. The studies alternate between historic and didactic, in order that the prophecies may be taken, as far as possible, in-relation to the history. Outlines of the prophecies are found in "Analyzed Bible," and the messages from the first volume of "The Messages of the Books of the Bible."

Wonderful as the prophetic voices were, none was complete, neither was final truth on any of these matters of government and grace revealed by the whole of them. In the Gospel according to Luke we see the Word of God final on all these subjects through "Jesus. . .the Son of Adam, the Son of God." In teaching we must observe how, the need revealed in the Old Testament has been met in Christ.

THE BIBLE IN FIVE YEARS

A. HISTORIC AND PROPHETIC STUDIES

FOURTH YEAR

HISTORIC AND DIDACTIC STUDIES. THE GOSPELS

THE GOSPEL ACCORDING TO JOHN

INTRODUCTORY NOTE

THE FIRST SECTION of the lessons for this year deals with the history of Jesus the Christ; and with His teaching. In previous years the first three records, Matthew, Mark, and Luke, have been considered in their special setting forth of some aspect of the Person and work of our Lord. Now the endeavor should be to study the historic sequence, setting the teaching of the Lord in relation to His doing.

The authority of the King, of the Priest, of the Prophet is such as to create wonder and inquiry. Here is the peculiar value of the Gospel according to John. This book consists of a grouping of incidents and of teachings, and their setting in such inter-relationship as to present one supreme fact concerning the Person of the Lord, that He is the Son of God. These lessons are condensed from Analyzed Bible.

A. HISTORIC AND DIDACTIC STUDIES. THE GOSPELS

Group I. Historic. The Christ, The Man, and the Ministry. Initiation.

LESSON 1. The Signs of His Coming.

Luke 1:5-56

Matthew 1:18-25

Luke 1:57-80

LESSON 2. The Days of His Flesh. The Man

Luke 2:1-38

Matthew 2:1-12.

Matthew 2:13-23

Luke 2:39-51 Mark 1:2-13

Matthew 3-4:11

Luke 2:52-4:13

John 1:19-36

LESSON 3. The Days of His Flesh. The Ministry. Initiation.

John 1:35-3:36

LESSON 4. The Days of His Flesh. The Ministry. Initiation.

John 4, 5

Group II. Teaching During First Period of Ministry.

LESSON 5. Preliminary, and First Discussion.

John 1:38, 39, 42, 47-51

John 2:4, 6, 19; 3:2-21

LESSON 6. Second and Third Discussions, and First Teaching of Disciples.

John 4:7-26, 32-38

John 5:17-47

Group III . Historic. The Ministry. Proclamation.

LESSON 7. First Journeyings, Calling of Disciples, and Manifesto.

Mark 1:14, 15

Matthew 4:12

Luke 4:14, 15

Luke 4:16-30

Mark 1:16-20

Matthew 4:18-22

Mark 1:21a

Matthew 4:13-17

Luke 4:31a

Mark 1:21b-39

Matthew 8:14-17 and 4:23-25

Luke 4:31b-44

Luke 5:1-11

Matthew 5-7

Mark 1:40-45

Matthew 8:1-4

Luke 5:12-16

Mark 2:1-22

Matthew 9:1-17

Luke 5:17-39.

Mark 2:23-3:6

Matthew 7:1-14

Luke 6:1-11

Mark 3:7-12

Matthew 12:15-21

LESSON 8. Appointment of Twelve, and Second Journeyings.

Mark 3:13-19a

Luke 6:12-16

Luke 6:17-49

Matthew 8:5-13

Luke 7:1-10

Luke 7:11-17

Matthew 11:2-19

Luke 7:18-35

Matthew 11:20-30

Luke 7:36-8:3

Mark 3:19b-21

Mark 3:20-30

Matthew 12:22-37

Luke 11:14, 15 and 17-23

Matthew 12:38-45

Luke 11:16 and 24-26

Luke 11:27, 28

Mark 3:31-4:34

Matthew 12:46-13:35

Luke 8:4-19

Matthew 13:36-52

Matthew 8:18-22

Luke 9:57-60

Mark 4:35-v.43

Matthew 8:23-9:20

Luke 8:22-56

Matthew 9:27-34

Mark 6:1-6

Matthew 8:54-58

LESSON 9. Mission of the Twelve, Third Journeying, and Confession of Peter.

Mark 6:7-13

Matthew 9:35-11:1

Luke 9:1-6.

Mark 6:14-31

Matthew 14:1-13

Luke 9:7-l0a

Mark 6:32-46

Matthew xiv. 14-23

Luke 9:10b-17 and John 6:1-15

Mark 6:47-56

Matthew 14:24-36

John 6:16-21

John 6:22-7:1

Mark 7:1-30

Matthew 15:1-28

Mark 7:31-37

Matthew 15:29-31

Mark 8:1-21

Matthew 15:32-16:12

Mark 8:22-26

Mark 8:27-9:1

Matthew 16:13-28

Luke 9:18-27

Group IV. Teaching During Second Period of Ministry.

LESSON 10. The Messianic Ministry, Claim, and Manifesto. Mainly Ethical.

Matthew 4:17

Mark 1:14, 15

Luke 4:18-27

Matthew 5-7

LESSON 11. Incidental Teaching on His Journeys.

Matthew 9:1-17

Mark 2:1-22

Luke 5:17-39

Matthew 7:1-14

Mark 2:23-3:6

Luke 6:1-11

Luke 6:20-49

LESSON 12. Incidental Teaching on His Journeys.

Matthew 8:5-13

Luke 7:1-10

Matthew 11:2-19

Luke 7:18-35

Matthew 11:20-30

Luke 7:39-50

Matthew 12:22-50

Mark 3:22-35

Luke 11:14-32 and 8:19-21

LESSON 13. The Parables, and Charge to the Twelve.

Matthew 13:1-23

Mark 4:1-20

Luke 8:4-15

Mark 4:21-25

Luke 8:16-18

Mark 4:26-29

Matthew 13:24-30

Matthew 13:31-32

Mark 4:30-32

Matthew 13:33

Matthew 13:34-35

Mark 4:33-34

Matthew 13:36-52

Matthew 10:1-15

Mark 6:7-11

Luke 90:1-5

Matthew 10:16-11:1

Mark 6:12, 13

Luke 9:6

LESSON 14. Parabolic Instruction and Warning.

John 6:26-71.

Matthew 15:1-20

Mark 7:1-23.

Matthew 16:1-12

Mark 8:11-21

LESSON 15. The Climax. Casarea Philippi.

Matthew 16:18-28

Mark 8:31-9:1

Luke 9:22-27.

Group V. Historic, The Ministry. Consurnmation.

LESSON 16. Preliminary, and the Progress to the End.

Mark 9:2-10:1

Matthew 17-19:2

Luke 9:28-50

John 7:2-10

Luke 9:51-56 and 61, 62

John 7:11-8:59

Luke 10

John 9-10:21

Luke 11-13:21

John 10:22-39

LESSON 17. Progress to the End, and the Last Stage.

John 10:40-42

Luke 13:22-17:10

John 11:1-54

Luke 17:11-19

Mark 10:2-52

Matthew 19:3-20:34

Luke 11:1-13 and 33-54

LESSON 21. Teaching in the Presence of the Multitudes.

Luke 12-13:9

LESSON 22. Public Discussions.

Luke 13:10-21

John 10:25-38

Luke 13:23-14:24

LESSON 23. Public Discussions.

Luke 14:25-16:13

LESSON 24. Public Discussion, Private Instruction of Disciples, and Teaching Connected with the Final Sign.

Luke 16:14-17:10

John 11:4-44

LESSON 25. Public Discussions and Private Instruction of Disciples.

Luke 17:20-18:14

Matthew 19:3-14

Mark 10:2-15

Luke 18:16, 17

Matthew 19:23-30

Mark 10:23-31

Luke 18:24-30

Matthew 20:1-16

Matthew 20:17-28

Mark 10:32-45

Luke 18:31-34

Luke 19:11-27

Group VII. Historic. The Christ. Death and the Signs of His Power.

LESSON 26. The Supper, Jesus and the Hebrew Nation, Jesus and His Own.

Mark 14:3-9

Matthew 26:6-13

John 12:2-11

Mark 11-12:12

Matthew 21:1-46

Luke 19:29-20:19 and John 12:12-19

Matthew 22:1-14

Mark 12:13-40

Matthew 22:15-23:12

Luke 20:20-47

Mark 12:41-44

Luke 21:1-4

Matthew 23:13-39

John 12:20-50

Mark 13:1-37

Matthew 24:1-44

Luke 21:5-36.

Matthew 24:45-26:2

Mark 14:1, 2, 10-17

Matthew 26:2-5, 14-19

Luke 221-6, 7-13

John 13:1

Luke 22:14-18

John 13:2-20

Mark 14:18-21

Matthew 26:20-24

Luke 22:21-23 and John 13:21-30

Mark 14:22-25

Matthew 26:26-29

Luke 22:19, 20 and 24-38

John 13:31-14:31a

Mark 14:26

Matthew 26:30

John 14:31b

John 15-17

Mark 14:27-31

Matthew 26:31-35

LESSON27. Jesus Himself, and the Signs of His Power.

Mark 14:32-15

Matthew 26:36-27

Luke 22:39-23

John 18:19

Mark 16

Matthew 28

Luke 24

John 20:21

Group VIII. The Final Earthly Teaching.

LESSON 28. Denunciatory. The Hebrew Nation.

Matthew 21:18-22

Mark 11:12-14 and 22-25

Matthew 21:23-22:46

Mark 11:27-12:37 and Luke 20:1-44

Matthew 23:1-12

Mark 12:38-44

Luke 20:45-21:4

Matthew 23:13-39

John 12:23-36

LESSON 29. Consolatory. His Own.

Matthew 24:1-44

Mark 13:1-37

Luke 21:5-36

Matthew 24:45-25

LESSON 30. Consolatory. His Own.

John 13-16

LESSON 31. The Prayer of the Word, The Words from the Cross, and Teaching after Resurrection.

John 17

Luke 23:34a, 39-43

John 19:25-27

Matthew 27:46.47

Mark 15:34.35

Matthew 27:48, 49

Mark 15:36

Matthew 27:50a

Mark 15:37a

Luke 23:46a, and John 19:30a

Luke 23:46b

Luke 24:13-27

Mark 16:15-18

Luke 24:36-49

John 20:19-29

John 21:15-23

Matthew 28:18-20

Acts 1:6-12

B. THE GOSPEL ACCORDING TO JOHN

LESSON 32. Jesus Christ the Word of God, From Everlasting. 1:1-18

LESSON 33. God manifest, in the World. Prologue, and Initial Signs and Wonders. 1:19-4

LESSON 34. God manifest, in the World. The Formal Showing. Of Life. 5-7:52

LESSON 35. God manifest, in the World. The Formal Showing. Of Light and Love. 7:53-10

FIFTH YEAR

HISTORIC STUDIES. THE CHURCH
APOSTOLIC LETTERS
THE APOCALYPSE

INTRODUCTORY NOTE

THE FIRST SEVEN lessons are devoted in this last year to the history found in the book of the Acts, thus following immediately upon that of the Gospel narratives.

The principle of the grouping of the apostolic letters is that of the general character of the epistles, indicated by the terms fundamental, experimental, and vocational. By fundamental is meant those in which the great doctrines of the faith are more definitely stated. By experimental is meant those in which the Christian experience is the prominent note. By vocational is meant those in which the function of the Church is more distinctly dealt with. The content of each epistle is reproduced from the Analyzed Bible; and the message from the second volume of "The Messages of the Books of the Bible."

The connection of the last book of the Bible with the subjects already taken in the present year, is that it completes the apostolic outlook. This began with the incarnation, life, death, resurrection, and ascension of our Lord. It then had to do with Pentecost and the Church in the first generation of its history. It also supplied the writings necessary for the instruction of the Church to the end of the age. Here the burden of the revelation is that of the things beyond the consummation of the age.

A. HISTORIC STUDIES. THE CHURCH

LESSON 1. In Jerusalem. Acts 2:5-8:3

LESSON 2. In Judaa and Samaria. To the Uttermost Part of the Earth. Toward Africa. In Asia. Acts 8:4-12:24

LESSON 3. To the Uttermost Part of the Earth. In Asia. Acts 12:25-16:8

LESSON 4. To the Uttermost Part of the Earth. In Europe. In Asia. Acts 16:9-20:1

LESSON 5. To the Uttermost Part of the Earth. In Europe. In Asia. Acts 20:2-23

LESSON 6. To the Uttermost Part of the Earth. In Asia. Events in Casarea. In Europe. Acts 24-28

LESSON 7. Subsequent Events in Paul's History. Other Historic References.

Titus 1:5; 3:12

1 Timothy 1:3

2 Timothy 1:15, 16, 17; 2:9; 4:10, 13; 14:20

1 Peter 5:12

Revelation 1:9

B. APOSTOLIC LETTERS.

Group I. The Fundamental Letters.

LESSON 8. Romans. 1-5

LESSON 9. Romans. 6-11

LESSON 10. Romans. 12-16

LESSON 11. Galatians.

LESSON 12. I Thessalonians.

LESSON 13. 2 Thessalonians.

LESSON 14. Hebrews. 1-4:13

LESSON 15. Hebrews. 4:14-10:39

LESSON 16. Hebrews. 10:38-13

LESSON 17. The Letters of John.

Group II. The Experimental Letters.

LESSON 18. Philippians

LESSON 19. 1 Peter

LESSON 20. 2 Peter

LESSON 21. James

LESSON 22. Philemon and Jude

Group III. The Vocational Letters.

LESSON 23. 1 Corinthians 1-11

C. THE APOCALYPSE.

About CrossReach Publications

CROSSREACH PUBLICATIONS

Thank you for choosing <u>CrossReach Publications</u>.

Hope. Inspiration. Trust.

These three words sum up the philosophy of why CrossReach Publications exist. To creating inspiration for the present thus inspiring hope for the future, through trusted authors from previous generations.

We are *non-denominational* and *non-sectarian*. We appreciate and respect what every part of the body brings to the table and believe everyone has the right to study and come to their own conclusions. We aim to help facilitate that end.

We aspire to excellence. If we have not met your standards please contact us and let us know. We want you to feel satisfied with your product. Something for everyone. We publish quality books both in presentation and content from a wide variety of authors who span various doctrinal positions and traditions, on a wide variety of Christian topics that will teach, encourage, challenge, inspire and equip.

We're a family-based home-business. A husband and wife team raising 8 kids. If you have any questions or comments about our publications email us at:

CrossReach@outlook.com

Don't forget you can follow us on <u>Facebook</u> and <u>Twitter</u>, (links are on the copyright page above) to keep up to date on our newest titles and deals.

Bestselling Titles from Crossreach

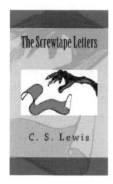

<u>The Screwtape Letters</u>
C. S. Lewis
$7.99
www.amazon.com/dp/1535260181

I have no intention of explaining how the correspondence which I now offer to the public fell into my hands.

There are two equal and opposite errors into which our race can fall about the devils. One is to disbelieve in their existence. The other is to believe, and to feel an excessive and unhealthy interest in them. They themselves are equally pleased by both errors and hail a materialist or a magician with the same delight. The sort of script which is used in this book can be very easily obtained by anyone who has once learned the knack; but ill-disposed or excitable people who might make a bad use of it shall not learn it from me.

Readers are advised to remember that the devil is a liar. Not everything that Screwtape says should be assumed to be true even from his own angle. I have made no attempt to identify any of the human beings mentioned in the letters; but I think it very unlikely that the portraits, say, of Fr. Spike or the patient's mother, are wholly just. There is wishful thinking in Hell as well as on Earth.

A Grief Observed
C. S. Lewis
$6.99
www.amazon.com/dp/1534898409

No one ever told me that grief felt so like fear. I am not afraid, but the sensation is like being afraid. The same fluttering in the stomach, the same restlessness, the yawning. I keep on swallowing. At other times it feels like being mildly drunk, or concussed. There is a sort of invisible blanket between the world and me. I find it hard to take in what anyone says. Or perhaps, hard to want to take it in. It is so uninteresting. Yet I want the others to be about me. I dread the moments when the house is empty. If only they would talk to one another and not to me.

How to Be Filled with the Holy Spirit
A. W. Tozer
$9.99
www.amazon.com/dp/1517462282

Before we deal with the question of how to be filled with the Holy Spirit, there are some matters which first have to be settled. As believers you have to get them out of the way, and right here is where the difficulty arises. I have been afraid that my listeners might have gotten the idea somewhere that I had a how-to-be-filled-with-the-Spirit-in-five-easy-lessons doctrine, which I could give you. If you can have any such vague ideas as that, I can only stand before you and say, "I am sorry"; because it isn't true; I can't give you such a course. There are some things, I say, that you have to get out of the way, settled.

"In his work on "The Two Babylons" Dr. Hislop has proven conclusively that all the idolatrous systems of the nations had their origin in what was founded by that mighty Rebel, the beginning of whose kingdom was Babel (Gen. 10:10)."—A. W. Pink, The Antichrist (1923)

There is this great difference between the works of men and the works of God, that the same minute and searching investigation, which displays the defects and imperfections of the one, brings out also the beauties of the other. If the most finely polished needle on which the art of man has been expended be subjected to a microscope, many inequalities, much roughness and clumsiness, will be seen. But if the microscope be brought to bear on the flowers of the field, no such result appears. Instead of their beauty diminishing, new beauties and still more delicate, that have escaped the naked eye, are forthwith discovered; beauties that make us appreciate, in a way which otherwise we could have had little conception of, the full force of the Lord's saying, "Consider the lilies of the field, how they grow; they toil not, neither do they spin: and yet I say unto you, That even Solomon, in all his glory, was not arrayed like one of these." The same law appears also in comparing the Word of God and the most finished productions of men. There are spots and blemishes in the most admired productions of human genius. But the more the Scriptures are searched, the more minutely they are studied, the more their perfection appears; new beauties are brought into light every day; and the discoveries of science, the researches of the learned, and the labours of infidels, all alike conspire to illustrate the wonderful harmony of all the parts, and the Divine beauty that clothes the whole. If this be the case with Scripture in general, it is especially the case with prophetic Scripture. As every spoke in the wheel of Providence revolves, the prophetic symbols start into still more bold and beautiful relief. This is very strikingly the case with the prophetic language that forms the groundwork and corner-stone of the present work. There never has been any difficulty in the mind of any enlightened Protestant in identifying the woman "sitting on seven mountains," and having on her forehead the name written, "Mystery, Babylon the Great," with the Roman apostacy.

The Person and Work of the Holy Spirit
R. A. Torey
$5.75
www.amazon.com/dp/1533030308

BEFORE one can correctly understand the work of the Holy Spirit, he must first of all know the Spirit Himself. A frequent source of error and fanaticism about the work of the Holy Spirit is the attempt to study and understand His work without first of all coming to know Him as a Person.

It is of the highest importance from the standpoint of worship that we decide whether the Holy Spirit is a Divine Person, worthy to receive our adoration, our faith, our love, and our entire surrender to Himself, or whether it is simply an influence emanating from God or a power or an illumination that God imparts to us. If the Holy Spirit is a person, and a Divine Person, and we do not know Him as such, then we are robbing a Divine Being of the worship and the faith and the love and the surrender to Himself which are His due.

The Problem of Pain
C. S. Lewis
$6.99
www.amazon.com/dp/1535052120

When Mr. Ashley Sampson suggested to me the writing of this book, I asked leave to be allowed to write it anonymously, since, if I were to say what I really thought about pain, I should be forced to make statements of such apparent fortitude that they would become ridiculous if anyone knew who made them. Anonymity was rejected as inconsistent with the series; but Mr. Sampson pointed out that I could write a preface explaining that I did not live up to my own principles! This exhilarating programme I am now carrying out. Let me confess at once, in the words of good Walter Hilton, that throughout this book "I feel myself so far from true feeling of that I speak, that I can naught else but cry mercy and desire after it as I may". Yet for that very reason there is one criticism which cannot be brought against me. No one can say "He jests at scars who never felt a wound", for I have never for one moment been in a state of mind to which even the imagination of serious pain was less than intolerable. If any man is safe from the danger of under-estimating this adversary, I am that man. I must add, too, that the only purpose of the book is to solve the intellectual problem raised by suffering; for the far higher task of teaching fortitude and patience I was never fool enough to suppose myself qualified, nor have I anything to offer my readers except my conviction that when pain is to be borne, a little courage helps more than much knowledge, a little human sympathy more than much courage, and the least tincture of the love of God more than all.

Out of the Silent Planet
C. S. Lewis
$7.92
www.amazon.com/dp/1536869929

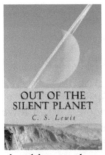

The last drops of the thundershower had hardly ceased falling when the Pedestrian stuffed his map into his pocket, settled his pack more comfortably on his tired shoulders, and stepped out from the shelter of a large chestnut-tree into the middle of the road. A violent yellow sunset was pouring through a rift in the clouds to westward, but straight ahead over the hills the sky was the colour of dark slate. Every tree and blade of grass was dripping, and the road shone like a river. The Pedestrian wasted no time on the landscape but set out at once with the determined stride of a good walker who has lately realized that he will have to walk farther than he intended. That, indeed, was his situation. If he had chosen to look back, which he did not, he could have seen the spire of Much Nadderby, and, seeing it, might have uttered a malediction on the inhospitable little hotel which, though obviously empty, had refused him a bed. The place had changed hands since he last went for a walking-tour in these parts. The kindly old landlord on whom he had reckoned had been replaced by someone whom the barmaid referred to as 'the lady,' and the lady was apparently a British innkeeper of that orthodox school who regard guests as a nuisance. His only chance now was Sterk, on the far side of the hills, and a good six miles away. The map marked an inn at Sterk. The Pedestrian was too experienced to build any very sanguine hopes on this, but there seemed nothing else within range.

Claiming Our Rights
E. W. Kenyon
$7.99
www.amazon.com/dp/1522757481

There is no excuse for the spiritual weakness and poverty of the Family of God when the wealth of Grace and Love of our great Father with His power and wisdom are all at our disposal. We are not coming to the Father as a tramp coming to the door begging for food; we come as sons not only claiming our legal rights but claiming the natural rights of a child that is begotten in love. No one can hinder us or question our right of approach to our Father.

Satan has Legal Rights over the sinner that God cannot dispute or challenge. He can sell them as slaves; he owns them, body, soul and spirit. But the moment we are born again... receive Eternal Life, the nature of God,—his legal dominion ends.

Christ is the Legal Head of the New Creation, or Family of God, and all the Authority that was given Him, He has given us: (Matthew 28:18), "All authority in heaven," the seat of authority, and "on earth," the place of execution of authority. He is "head over all things," the highest authority in the Universe, for the benefit of the Church which is His body.

Home Geography for the Primary Grades
C. C. Long
$7.95
www.amazon.com/dp/1518780660

A popular homeschooling resource for many generations now. Geography may be divided into the geography of the home and the geography of the world at large. A knowledge of the home must be obtained by direct observation; of the rest of the world, through the imagination assisted by information. Ideas acquired by direct observation form a basis for imagining those things which are distant and unknown. The first work, then, in geographical instruction, is to study that small part of the earth's surface lying just at our doors. All around are illustrations of lake and river, upland and lowland, slope and valley. These forms must be actually observed by the pupil, mental pictures obtained, in order that he may be enabled to build up in his mind other mental pictures of similar unseen forms. The hill that he climbs each day may, by an appeal to his imagination, represent to him the lofty Andes or the Alps. From the meadow, or the bit of level land near the door, may be developed a notion of plain and prairie. The little stream that flows past the schoolhouse door, or even one formed by the sudden shower, may speak to him of the Mississippi, the Amazon, or the Rhine. Similarly, the idea of sea or ocean may be deduced from that of pond or lake. Thus, after the pupil has acquired elementary ideas by actual perception, the imagination can use them in constructing, on a larger scale, mental pictures of similar objects outside the bounds of his own experience and observation.

In His Steps
Charles M. Sheldon
$3.99
www.amazon.com/dp/1535086262

The sermon story, In His Steps, or "What Would Jesus Do?" was first written in the winter of 1896, and read by the author, a chapter at a time, to his Sunday evening congregation in the Central Congregational Church, Topeka, Kansas. It was then printed as a serial in The Advance (Chicago), and its reception by the readers of that paper was such that the publishers of The Advance made arrangements for its appearance in book form. It was their desire, in which the author heartily joined, that the story might reach as many readers as possible, hence succeeding editions of paper-covered volumes at a price within the reach of nearly all readers.

The story has been warmly and thoughtfully welcomed by Endeavor societies, temperance organizations, and Y. M. C. A. 's. It is the earnest prayer of the author that the book may go its way with a great blessing to the churches for the quickening of Christian discipleship, and the hastening of the Master's kingdom on earth.

Charles M. Sheldon.
Topeka, Kansas,
November, 1897.

Made in United States
Troutdale, OR
04/27/2024

19493996R00040